BE A SMART CLIENT

WORKBOOK

For Your

Personal Injury Case

(Your Name Here)

ALSO BY THE AUTHOR

Be A Smart Client

Adventures With Natural Healing

Re-Energize Yourself

Home Office Handbook

Government Auctions/Sales Manual

105 Ways To Make Money At Home

Dental Heaven

Office Wizard -
Office Procedures Manual Software Template

And more...

Visit

www.TheMcKeeCompany.com

The McKee Company
www.BeASmartClient.com
P.O. Box 22996, Denver, CO 80222
contact@themckeecompany.com
(303) 719-2154
Copyright ©2015 The McKee Company

 BONUS ONLINE CONTENT: For more resources, visit our website: www.BeASmartClient.com.

ISBN-13: 978-1514623442
ISBN-10: 1514623447

FIRST EDITION

Disclaimer

The information contained herein should not be taken as legal advice. The author was a career paralegal. The views expressed in here and website www.BeASmartClient.com are those of the author alone.

TABLE OF CONTENTS

This workbook is to be used by anyone who has suffered an injury due to another's negligence and is seeking compensation. Keeping your case details in one place will help things progress more smoothly, with step-by-step assistance throughout your case.

For explanation regarding certain requested information or instructions on handling specific situations, refer to the book, **Be A Smart Client**.

INSTRUCTIONS

Thank you for using the **Be A Smart Client** workbook. You will find it easy to use, comprehensive and logical. It will help you keep everything in one place so you can find things quickly.

In addition to this workbook, you will need a few other items:

- ✓ Large (8 X 10) envelope to hold receipts
- ✓ File folder to hold hard copies of letters from attorney and letters you wrote to them
- ✓ File folder to hold court documents received from attorney OR a 3-ring binder
- ✓ File folder for copies of documents given to attorney (*See Record on Page 39*)

◊ Label each file folder so you can tell at a glance what it holds.

◊ Fill out Chapter 1 <u>first</u> - Details of Your Case.

◊ Fill in all sections as *completely as possible, as soon as possible*. The longer you wait, the more details will be forgotten.

◊ If you need more room to write your answers, use the blank pages starting on Page 42.

The book **Be A Smart Client** will answer any questions regarding topics covered in this companion workbook. *It is recommended you use the book in conjunction with this workbook.*

1

▶DETAILS OF YOUR CASE

First things first. You need to write a paragraph of what happened. The information you supply in the first five points will give you details to write a comprehensive statement. Please answer all questions completely.

▲ *Type of case*: *(check all that apply)*

___ Vehicle accident	___ Assault/battery	___ Defamation
___ Dog bite/Attack	___ Liable/Slander	___ Medical Malpractice
___ Nuisance	___ Nursing Home	___ Slip and fall
___ Trespass	___ Wrongful Death	
___ Other (*describe*) _____		

▲ *Specifics:*

Date/Time of Loss: _____

Location of Loss: _____

Weather conditions: _____

▲ *Parties involved:*

_____

Name   *Contact Info*   *Description (Height, weight, facial hair, eye color, tattoos, etc.)*

_____

Name   *Contact Info*   *Description*

_____

Name   *Contact Info*   *Description*

_____

Name   *Contact Info*   *Description*

Use blank pages starting on Page 42 if more room is needed.

▲ *Vehicles involved:* (if applicable)

Make/Model of other vehicle(s): _____

Description of other vehicle(s): _____

License plate, color, year, bumper stickers, signage

_____

_____

▲ *Your losses:* (check all that apply)

____ Physical   ____ Monetary   ____ Emotional/Mental

▲ *Comprehensive Statement of Incident*

Describe the event in detail using your answers to previous ▲ points.

_____

_____

_____

_____

_____

_____

_____

_____

_____

_____

_____

_____

_____

_____

_____

_____

_____

_____

_____

▲ *Basic Statement of Incident*

Write an abbreviated version of your comprehensive statement describing only <u>Who</u> did <u>What</u> to you and <u>How</u> it changed your life.

_____

_____

_____

_____

_____

▲ *What are your goals?*

What would it take to make you whole? What would it take to return you to the position you were before the injury? What has this incident cost you in terms of money, time, pain? Include all monetary damages you can calculate at this time (*medical treatment, lost wages, repair and earning capacity, replacement of damaged property*). Future money values will be determined later.

_____

_____

_____

_____

_____

_____

_____

_____

_____

_____

_____

_____

Use blank pages starting on Page 42 if more room is needed.

2

► BACKGROUND

This is basic information an attorney requires. Most lawyers provide a more detailed questionnaire, but until you receive one, this will get you started.

▲ *Personal Information*

List all other names by which you have ever been known, including marital and maiden names, nicknames, and aliases:

_____

_____

Home Address: _____

Prior addresses in the past 3 years and length of stay:

_____

_____

_____

Cell Phone: _____ Work Phone: _____ Home Phone: _____

Date of Birth: _____ Birthplace (*city/ state/ country*): _____

Are you married? Yes ____ No ____

    If yes, Date of Marriage: _____

Place of Marriage: _____

Spouse's Name: _____

Spouse's Phone: _____

Please list the name, age, relationship and address of everyone, including children, who are dependent upon you for support.

Name: _____ Age: _____

Relationship: _____ Address: _____

Name: _____ Age: _____
Relationship: _____Address: _____

Name: _____ Age: _____
Relationship: _____Address: _____

Name: _____ Age: _____
Relationship: _____Address: _____

Name: _____ Age: _____
Relationship: _____Address: _____

▲ *Employment Information*

Current or Most Recent Employer: _____

Employer Address: _____

Beginning Date: _____Ending Date: _____ Position: _____
Job Description: _____
Beginning Pay Rate: _____ Current or Last Pay Rate: _____
Have you ever missed work due to your injuries? Yes _____ No _____

   If yes, list dates you were unable to work. From: _____ To: _____

Reason for leaving. (*If you still work here, write N/A*) :

_____

_____

Prior Employer: _____
Employer Address: _____

Beginning Date: _____Ending Date: _____ Position: _____
Job Description: _____
Beginning Pay Rate: _____ Current or Last Pay Rate: _____
Have you ever missed work due to your injuries? Yes _____ No _____

   If yes, list dates you were unable to work. From: _____ To: _____

Reason for leaving :

_____

_____

▲ *Education*

List your highest educational level (high school, college, graduate school, professional training): _____

Name of Institution: _____

Address: _____

Do you have any special job training? Yes ____ No ____

 If yes, please describe: _____

▲ *Military*

Have you ever been in the military? Yes ____ No ____

 If yes, Dates of Service: _____

 If no, go to next section - Prior Claims and Lawsuits

Service Number: _____ Branch: _____

Type of Discharge: _____

Have you had any service-related injuries/disabilities? Yes ____ No ____

 If yes, please describe: _____

_____

_____

_____

Disability %: _____ Present condition of accident-related injury/disability:

_____

Do you receive payments for these injuries? Yes ____ No ____

 If yes, please provide: Amount _____ Frequency _____

 Source (Veterans, Social Security, Private Insurance, Other)

_____

▲ *Prior Claims and Lawsuits*

Please list every claim you have ever made for personal injury or property damage (*use blank pages starting on Page 42 if necessary*).

Date: _____ Nature of Claim: _____

Against Whom: _____

Result: _____

_____

Please list every claim you have ever made for personal injury or property damage.

Date: _____ Nature of Claim: _____

Against Whom: _____

Result: _____

_____

Please list every claim you have ever made for personal injury or property damage.

Date: _____ Nature of Claim: _____

Against Whom: _____

Result: _____

_____

▲ *Prior Accidents and Injuries*

Please list **all** prior accidents, whether they resulted in a claim for damages or not. Failure to mention other accidents or injuries can undermine a lawsuit, no matter how minor they may seem.

Date: _____

Location: _____

Nature of Accident: _____

Extent of Injuries: _____

Date: _____

Location: _____

Nature of Accident: _____

Extent of Injuries: _____

Date: _____

Location: _____

Nature of Accident: _____

Extent of Injuries: _____

Date: _____

Location: _____

Nature of Accident: _____

Extent of Injuries: _____

Date: _____

Location: _____

Nature of Accident: _____

Extent of Injuries: _____

3

► SELECTING AND HIRING AN ATTORNEY

▲ *Personal Preferences*

Answer the following five questions, then call 3-5 attorneys who: 1) fit your preferences, and 2) work on your type of case.

⬤ BONUS ONLINE CONTENT: For steps to take and questions to ask when looking for an attorney, visit www.BeASmartClient.com.

◊ I feel more comfortable talking with: ___ Male ___ Female ___ No preference
◊ I prefer working with a lawyer who has been in practice: ___ Less than a year ___ 1-5 years ___ Over 5 years ___ No preference
◊ I am willing to travel _____ miles/minutes for appointments.
◊ I prefer to correspond by: (*choose all that apply in order of preference*) ___ Phone ___Email ___Text ___ Hard copy letters
◊ I prefer an attorney whose personality is ___ Very casual ___ Semi-Casual ___ Formal (*determine this during initial call*)

▲ *Initial Contact By Telephone*

After telling them your basic statement from Page 3, ask each attorney the following questions.

1st Attorney
How long have you been practicing law? _____

What is your field(s) of expertise? _____

Have you worked other cases similar to mine? ___ Yes ___ No
    If yes, approximately how many? _____
    If yes, what is your rate of success? _____
    If yes, I realize every case is different, but on the average, how
        long did they take to settle? _____

Do you think my case has merit? ___ Yes ___ No

Would you pursue this if you were me? ___ Yes ___ No *If no,* why not?
_____

What do you believe is the best case scenario? _____
_____

What do you believe is the worst case scenario? _____
_____

Do you have time to devote to my case? ___ Yes ___ No

Is there a deadline for filing my case? ___ Yes ___ No
    If yes, what is the deadline? _____

I prefer to correspond by (*see your answers on Page 10*).
How do you prefer to correspond? _____
How promptly do you return calls and e-mails? _____
How soon do you usually inform clients of actions you take? _____
What is your fee rate and how do you charge?
_____
What is your attorney registration number? _____

2nd Attorney
How long have you been practicing law? _____

What is your field(s) of expertise? _____

Have you worked other cases similar to mine? ___ Yes ___ No
    If yes, approximately how many? _____

If yes, what is your rate of success? _____

If yes, I realize every case is different, but on the average, how
  long did they take to settle? _____

Do you think my case has merit? ___ Yes ___ No

Would you pursue this if you were me? ___ Yes ___ No *If no,* why not?
_____

What do you believe is the best case scenario? _____
_____

What do you believe is the worst case scenario? _____
_____

Do you have time to devote to my case? ___ Yes ___ No

Is there a deadline for filing my case? ___ Yes ___ No

If yes, what is the deadline? _____

I prefer to correspond by (*see* your *answers on Page 10*).
How do you prefer to correspond? _____
How promptly do you return calls and e-mails? _____
How soon do you usually inform clients of actions you take? _____
What is your fee rate and how do you charge?
_____
What is your attorney registration number? _____

3rd Attorney
How long have you been practicing law? _____

What is your field(s) of expertise? _____

Have you worked other cases similar to mine? ___ Yes ___ No

If yes, approximately how many? _____

If yes, what is your rate of success? _____

If yes, I realize every case is different, but on the average, how
  long did they take to settle? _____

Do you think my case has merit? ___ Yes ___ No

Would you pursue this if you were me? ___ Yes ___ No *If no,* why not?
_____

What do you believe is the best case scenario? _____
_____

What do you believe is the worst case scenario? _____
_____

Do you have time to devote to my case? ___ Yes ___ No

Is there a deadline for filing my case? ___ Yes ___ No
      If yes, what is the deadline? _____

I prefer to correspond by (*see* your *answers on Page 10*).
How do you prefer to correspond? _____
How promptly do you return calls and e-mails? _____
How soon do you usually inform clients of actions you take? _____
What is your fee rate and how do you charge?
_____
What is your attorney registration number? _____

4th Attorney
How long have you been practicing law? _____

What is your field(s) of expertise? _____

Have you worked other cases similar to mine? ___ Yes ___ No
      If yes, approximately how many? _____
      If yes, what is your rate of success? _____
      If yes, I realize every case is different, but on the average, how
            long did they take to settle? _____
Do you think my case has merit? ___ Yes ___ No

Would you pursue this if you were me? ___ Yes ___ No *If no,* why not?
_____

What do you believe is the best case scenario? _____
_____

What do you believe is the worst case scenario? _____
_____

Do you have time to devote to my case? ___ Yes ___ No

Is there a deadline for filing my case? ___ Yes ___ No
    If yes, what is the deadline? _____

I prefer to correspond by (*see* your *answers on Page 10*).
How do you prefer to correspond? _____
How promptly do you return calls and e-mails? _____
How soon do you usually inform clients of actions you take? _____
What is your fee rate and how do you charge?
_____
What is your attorney registration number? _____

5th Attorney
How long have you been practicing law? _____

What is your field(s) of expertise? _____

Have you worked other cases similar to mine? ___ Yes ___ No
    If yes, approximately how many? _____
    If yes, what is your rate of success? _____
    If yes, I realize every case is different, but on the average, how
        long did they take to settle? _____
Do you think my case has merit? ___ Yes ___ No

Would you pursue this if you were me? ___ Yes ___ No *If no,* why not?
_____

What do you believe is the best case scenario? _____
_____

What do you believe is the worst case scenario? _____

_____

Do you have time to devote to my case? ___ Yes ___ No

Is there a deadline for filing my case? ___ Yes ___ No
    If yes, what is the deadline? _____

I prefer to correspond by (*see* your *answers on Page 10*).
How do you prefer to correspond? _____
How promptly do you return calls and e-mails? _____
How soon do you usually inform clients of actions you take? _____
What is your fee rate and how do you charge?

_____
What is your attorney registration number? _____

▲*Attorney Choices*

Review all conversations, answers to the above and list your top three attorney choices:

Attorney #1: _____
Attorney #2: _____
Attorney #3: _____

Use blank pages starting on Page 42 if more room is needed.

4

▶ PREPARATION FOR THE CONSULTATION

The first appointment is a fact-finding mission. Contact your top three attorneys from Page 8 and make an appointment with each for a consultation. The first meeting is often free. At this meeting you will share your goals on Page 4, how involved you want to be and how you expect billing, communication and paperwork to be handled.

▲ *Level of Involvement*

How involved do you want to be in your case?

____Not involved   ____Slightly Involved   ____ Very involved

◊ ***Not*** *involved: Provide what your attorney requests, keep your paperwork*
     organized. Keeping track of court dates is recommended.
◊ ***Slightly*** *involved: Run errands (delivery, copying) - plus everything above.*
◊ ***Very*** *involved: Perform research that does not require legal training - plus above.*

▲ *Expectations*

Good communication is key to any relationship. Read the Client Constitution and <u>check which points are important to you</u>. Discuss these with the attorney to confirm they agree to meet your expectations. (*See **How To Be A Smart Client** book for further explanation of these points.*)

*Points that indicate a higher level of involvement (*See Page 6*)

Client Constitution

___ I prefer to communicate with the same personnel throughout the case.

___If staffing changes occur, I will not be billed for time to educate new attorneys or staff about my case.

___I will receive prompt follow-up to my communications with attorney and staff. (*Ask the attorney their definition of "prompt"*)

___I expect efficient, timely completion of work, including keeping my file current and in good order.

___Meetings will be held during regular office hours unless cleared in advance with me.

___Only one lawyer and/or one staff member will attend meetings, hearings or other matters on my behalf.

___Hourly rates may not be increased without my prior approval.

___I will receive a monthly statement detailing description, timekeeper, time and costs.

___I will be kept current on case developments as soon as possible.

___I will be copied on all court-filed documents as soon as possible.

___I will be copied on all correspondence in relation to case.

___*I will be provided a schedule in advance of all court-appointed due dates (*depositions, discovery, etc.*).

___I will receive copies of invoices/receipts for items charged by outside vendors (*copies, postage, private investigator, etc.*).

___Invoices from outside vendors will be charged to me at face value.

___Messenger services and express mail shall be provided at cost and used only when an alternative is unavailable.

___Photocopying (in-house) may not exceed ___¢ per page (*10¢-15¢ is appropriate*).

___*If there is a large volume of documents, I will be given the opportunity to shop around for a price comparison.

___Before incurring any expense over $_____ (*not less than $50*), I will be contacted for approval before purchase is made.

___Before ordering medical or other records, attorney will verify and notify me if there is insurance or other asset to cover the cost.

___My approval will be needed for all travel expenses in advance.

___No local travel within 100 miles of office will be reimbursed.

The attorney will avoid:
___Overstaffing
___Frequent shuffling of assigned personnel

___Extensive "rework" of a written work product

___Handling specific tasks by persons who are either overqualified or underqualified

___Review of documents by multiple timekeepers

___Performing premature or minor legal or factual research

I will not be billed for:

___Internal conferences

___Internal notes or memorandum

___Scheduling meetings or depositions

___Research regarding simple issues which should already be within the knowledge of the firm

___Timekeeping

Other points you wish to discuss:

1. _____

2. _____

3. _____

BONUS ONLINE CONTENT: Increase your confidence by using the exercises listed under Confidence Builders at www.BeASmartClient.com.

5

►THE CONSULTATION

While you are assessing their qualities as an attorney, they are determining whether or not to accept you on as a client. Make a good first impression. Look and act as professional as possible.

▲ *Arrival*

✓ Call ahead for parking instructions
✓ Tell them if you have special needs for parking, office access, etc.
✓ Arrive on time
✓ Bring this workbook (*completed as much as possible*)
✓ Bring your driver's license or picture ID
✓ Bring accident report and/or legal documents (*if available*)
✓ Do not bring children or pets (*if possible; service animals excepted*)

▲ *Appearance*

✓ Clean clothes
✓ Clean hair and nails
✓ No cut-offs, sagging pants, ripped or revealing clothing
✓ Wear shoes
✓ Turn off or mute cell phone during appointment

▲ *Agenda*

✓ Give them your basic statement listed on Page 4.
✓ Discuss the Client Constitution and your expectations.
✓ Inform them how involved you want to be (*Page 16*).
✓ Discuss your goals from Page 4.
✓ Ask questions, take notes and review them before making a hiring decision.

▲ *Attitude*

- ✓ State the basic facts without emotion
- ✓ If you feel emotional, let a friend/relative help present the facts
- ✓ Show respect. Do not swear or tell jokes.

▲ *Fee Agreement*

Ask each attorney which method they use to charge clients

Atty. #1 ____Contingency Fee ____Hourly ____ Other _____

Atty. #2 ____Contingency Fee ____Hourly ____ Other _____

Atty. #3 ____Contingency Fee ____Hourly ____ Other _____

I have discussed the Client Constitution with the following attorneys and they agreed/disagreed to my expectations.

◊_____

Name of 1st attorney   Date   Agree/Disagree

If they disagreed, points they disagreed with: _____

_____.

◊_____

Name of 2nd attorney   Date   Agree/Disagree

If they disagreed, points they disagreed with: _____

_____.

◊_____

Name of 3rd attorney   Date   Agree/Disagree

If they disagreed, points they disagreed with: _____

_____.

Use blank pages starting on Page 42 if more room is needed.

6

▶ THE HIRING PROCESS

It is time to decide who to hire. You have interviewed at least three attorneys. Review your notes and list the pros and cons of each one. Hire whoever receives the most "Yes" answers.

1st Attorney Name: _____

Yes   No
___   ___   I feel comfortable talking with them.
___   ___   They explain things so I understand them.
___   ___   They have time to take on my case.
___   ___   They have experience in my type of case.
___   ___   They have been successful in my type of case.
___   ___   They agreed to my expectations in the Client Constitution.
___   ___   They agree to my preferred method of communication.
___   ___   They agree to my level of involvement.
___   ___   They have no disciplinary record.
___   ___   (Other)_____.

2nd Attorney Name: _____

Yes   No
___   ___   I feel comfortable talking with them.
___   ___   They explain things so I understand them.
___   ___   They have time to take on my case.
___   ___   They have experience in my type of case.
___   ___   They have been successful in my type of case.
___   ___   They agreed to my expectations in the Client Constitution.
___   ___   They agree to my preferred method of communication.
___   ___   They agree to my level of involvement.
___   ___   They have no disciplinary record.
___   ___   (Other)_____.

3rd Attorney Name: _____

Yes   No

___   ___   I feel comfortable talking with them.

___   ___   They explain things so I understand them.

___   ___   They have time to take on my case.

___   ___   They have experience in my type of case.

___   ___   They have been successful in my type of case.

___   ___   They agreed to my expectations in the Client Constitution.

___   ___   They agree to my preferred method of communication.

___   ___   They agree to my level of involvement.

___   ___   They have no disciplinary record.

___   ___   (*Other*)_____.

Use blank pages starting on Page 42 if more room is needed.

 BONUS ONLINE CONTENT: Different types of fee agreement can be found under Hiring Tips at www.BeASmartClient.com.

7

▶ INITIAL APPOINTMENT

Now that you have decided who to hire, contact them to set an appointment. At this meeting, take all documents you need to share with the attorney. Follow the same conduct rules listed on Page 19.

▲ *Items To Share With Attorney*

✓ Accident/Police report

✓ Insurance claim numbers

✓ Copy(ies) of your insurance policies

✓ Completed sections of this workbook, including:

   ❖ Comprehensive Statement on Page 2

   ❖ Goals on Page 4

   ❖ Background Information on Page 5

▲ *Items To Receive From/Discuss With Attorney*

✓ Fee Agreement (*read thoroughly before signing*)
✓ Agreement (*either verbal or written*) to selected Client Constitution points starting on Page 16.
✓ Attorney's Client Questionnaire

You have told the attorney what you expect from them. As you may imagine, they have expectations from you. You can ask them if they have specific requests, but the following are pretty standard. How you behave plays a big part in your case.

▲ *Client Responsibilities*

DO...

- ✓ Respond to all communication from attorney in a timely manner.
- ✓ Keep messages short and to the point.
- ✓ Dress appropriately for all meetings and/or court dates.
- ✓ Tell your attorney everything.
- ✓ Review all documents your attorney gives you.
- ✓ Carefully read all documents before signing them.
- ✓ Keep all paperwork organized.
- ✓ Keep original (*preferred*) or at least a copy of all documents you give attorney. (*Page 39*)
- ✓ Make sure your attorney has your current contact information.
- ✓ Pay your bill on time (*if applicable*).
- ✓ Let your attorney know as soon as possible if you will be late or need to cancel an appointment.
- ✓ Respect staff and their time.
- ✓ Turn your cell phone off or put on mute during appointments.

DO NOT...

- ✓ Leave repeated messages about the same issue.
- ✓ Leave several messages in one day unless it is an emergency. If You have several questions or concerns, consolidate them into one message.
- ✓ Show up at the office without an appointment.
- ✓ Bring children or pets to appointments.
- ✓ Lie to your attorney.
- ✓ Get personally involved with your attorney.
- ✓ Contact witnesses or others involved in your case without first informing attorney.

IT IS WISE TO...

✓ Take notes at meetings with your attorney.

✓ Ask the attorney if they have a designated time of day for accepting phone calls.

✓ Ask the attorney who to contact when you have non-legal questions such as paperwork, billing, etc.

✓ Have a good relationship with the office staff. Be professional, polite, and considerate.

✓ Keep your emotions in check when talking with the attorney.

✓ Make a copy of all documents you share with your attorney and give them the copies. **Keep the original whenever possible.**

✓ Start your diary as soon as possible after the incident.

✓ When reviewing documents from your attorney, use sticky notes or other means with defacing the document to easily locate important information.

✓ Verify contact details, especially email addresses

✓ Request your attorney verify insurance or other assets available before ordering expensive reports, such as medical records.

8

▶ DIARY

Remember, the more details you record, the better. You don't know what will be the "smoking gun" that could make or break your case.

▲ Conversations

Date/Time/ Location	Name/Relationship* (friend, witness, medical provider, etc.)	Detailed Description
5/6/14 9:30 am Doctor office	Karen/Physical therapist	30-minute therapy session. Karen said since heated water therapy wasn't working, next time she would try wax.

*Duplicate their name and contact information in Contact Log on Page 30 for quick retrieval.

Date/Time/ Location	Name/Relationship* (friend, witness, medical provider, etc.)	Detailed Description

*Duplicate their name and contact information in Contact Log on Page 30 for quick retrieval

Use pages starting on Page 42 if more room is needed

▲ *Thoughts*

Track your feelings to help others understand your frame of mind.

Date	*Mood* (angry, sad, depressed, etc.)	*Describe <u>why</u> you feel this way*
5/7/14	Depressed / Mad	Have to depend on Fran to get groceries for me; cannot do things for myself anymore. Feel helpless.

Use pages starting on Page 42 if more room is needed

▲ *Actions*

Keep track of how your life changed as a direct result of the incident.

Date	Description (doctor appointments, cannot attend social activity, pay others to do chores)
5/7	Pain was so bad, I could not attend graduation of nephew and first family reunion in 20 years.

Use pages starting on Page 42 if more room is needed

9

▶ CONTACTS

Record contact information for everyone you know related to your case who you spoke to before hiring a lawyer.

Name/Address	Phone	E-mail	Relationship (friend, witness, doctor, insurance agent, etc.)

Use pages starting on Page 42 if more room is needed

10

▶ **CALENDAR**

Record <u>court dates</u> supplied by your lawyer and <u>reminders</u> to contact people on this calendar.

Date	Item
6/14	Contact DMV if I haven't received accident report yet
7/30	Deadline for expert witness list

Date	Item

Use blank pages starting on Page 42 if more room is needed

11

► LOSS OF INCOME

If applicable, keep detailed notes regarding income lost <u>in addition to any regular job</u> due to the incident.

Date	Amount	Description
6/15	$100 estimate	Unable to give scheduled seminar - lost sales and possible contacts for other seminars

Use blank pages starting on Page 42 if more room is needed

12

▶ RECEIPTS

Keep receipts in envelope attached to back cover. Record receipts here.

Date	Amount	Description
6/19	$5.76	Probiotics to counteract the antibiotics - CVS - Walgreens

Date	Amount	Description
Total		

Use blank pages starting on Page 42 if more room is needed

13

▶ **COMMUNICATION**

▲ *Correspondence*

◊ *Letters*

Keep hard copy of letters and attachments (*both the ones you sent and received from attorney*) in one file folder in chronological order. (*See Page v*) Use the following sample form for letters you write regarding your case.

Your Name
Address
City, State and Zip Code
Email Address
Phone Number(s)

Date

Addressee

Re: Your Name
       Case No.: 12345
       Date of Loss: 7/26/11
       Defendant: Individual's Name

Dear (Mr./Mrs. Name or Sir/Madam):

Body of letter
(State the facts clearly and briefly. Be considerate and respectful. Get to the point immediately.)

Sincerely,

Your Name
(If you prefer, you can put your Address, and phone number under your name)

Enclosures - *List all enclosures*

    cc: *List all who are receiving a copy*
    bcc: *People you want to send a copy but keep them anonymous (cite only on your copy)*

◊ *E-Mails*

When sending an e-mail, **copy yourself** and move it to a separate email folder. Every time you send an email, ***change the Subject field to reflect the content.*** For example, the lawyer emails you and asks for an update on your physical therapy. When you reply, change the subject line to: "Answer to request for physical therapy update." A clearly defined subject line makes it is easy to find any email. **Always include your complete contact information on emails.**

◊ *Court-Filed Documents*

Keep these papers in a file or binder, most recent on top. (*See Page v*)

COURT CAPTION

District Court, Denver County, Colorado Court Address: 1447 17th Street Denver, CO 80202 720-555-5075　　　　　　　　　**(A)***	
James J. Doe, Plaintiff, v. Kyson Alan Mock, Defendant.　　　　　　　　　　　**(B)**	▲COURT USE ▲
Attorney or Party without Attorney: Michael Jones , Attorney Reg. No.: 1628165 P.O. Box 1125477 Denver, CO 80227 Phone: (720) 555-5303 E-mail: mjones@qabcz.com　　　　**(C)**	Case No: 1999CV490 **(D)** Division B
MOTION FOR CONTINUANCE	**(E)**

*Court Caption Key:
(A) Court address and phone number where case is filed
(B) Parties in case
(C) Attorney and contact information
(D) Year filed/Type of case/490th case filed in that year
　　　　(CR = Criminal, CV = Civil, PR = Probate)
(E) Title of document

◊ *Phone Calls*

Whenever possible, use a cell phone or VOIP (i.e. *Magic Jack*) because they automatically log date, time and duration of your calls. For calls that strongly impact your case (*changing a court date*), make a note of the date and time, who you talked to and the subject of the call in the table below.

Date/Time	Spoke to	Specifics of Conversation

Use blank pages starting on Page 42 if more room is needed

DOCUMENTS GIVEN TO ATTORNEY

Date	O/C*	Description of Document

*O = Original Document C = Copy

Use blank pages starting on Page 42 if more room is needed

14

▶RESEARCH NOTES

 An extensive list of research resources are listed in the book **Be A Smart Client.** An abbreviated list can be found at www.BeASmartClient.com.

Research Notes - Continued

CONTINUATION OF

_____ *(Section Name)*

CONTINUATION OF

_____ *(Section Name)*

CONTINUATION OF

_____ *(Section Name)*

_____ *(Section Name)*

CONTINUATION OF

_____ *(Section Name)*

CONTINUATION OF

_____ *(Section Name)*

CONTINUATION OF

_____ *(Section Name)*

Staple large envelope inside the back cover and keep all receipts in envelope. If receipt does not state what it is for, write on the back of receipt.